Photographic Memory

How to Improve Memory Skills and

Remember More of What You Read and Hear

By: Lawrence Franz

© Copyright 2018 - All rights reserved.

The contents of this book may not be reproduced, duplicated or transmitted without direct written permission from the author.

Under no circumstances will any legal responsibility or blame be held against the publisher for any reparation, damages, or monetary loss due to the information herein, either directly or indirectly.

Legal Notice:

This book is copyright protected. This is only for personal use. You cannot amend, distribute, sell, use, quote or paraphrase any part of the content within this book without the consent of the author.

Disclaimer Notice:

Please note the information contained within this document is for educational and entertainment purposes only. Every attempt has been made to provide accurate, up to date and complete, reliable information. No warranties of any kind are expressed or implied. Readers acknowledge that the author is not engaging in the rendering of legal, financial, medical or professional advice. The content of this book has been derived from various sources. Please consult a licensed professional before attempting any techniques outlined in this book.

By reading this document, the reader agrees that under no circumstances is the author responsible for any losses, direct or indirect, which are incurred as a result of the use of information contained within this document, including, but not limited to, —errors, omissions, or inaccuracies.

Table of Contents

Introduction 5
Chapter One: The Human Brain and Memory 13
   Short-Term Memory 14
   Long-Term Memory 17
   Encoding and Consolidation 20
   Memory and Emotions 24
   Recalling Memories from the Recesses of the Brain 26
Chapter Two: Creative Thinking and Visualization for Memory 28
Chapter Three: Peg System Memory Techniques 35
   How Does the Peg System Work 38
   The Number-Rhyme Peg System 39
   The Number-Shape Peg System 42
   Alphabet Peg System 43
Chapter Four: Tips to Remember Names 46
Chapter Five: Mind Mapping Tips 53
Chapter Six: Memory Palace 61
Chapter Seven: General Tips for Improved Memory 69
   Powerful Memory-Boosting Mental Exercises 69
   Lifestyle-Related Memory-Boosting Tips 73
   More Memory Building Tips 82
Conclusion 87

Introduction

Memory is a fascinating aspect of human beings and experts are still grappling with the effort of understanding in how many different mindboggling ways our brains work when it comes to storing and recalling data. Scientists are struggling to comprehend how some memories remain fresh long after the data has been assimilated into the brain while other memories are forgotten almost immediately after the event is over.

Photographic memory also referred to as eidetic memory, is the ability of the brain to recall any situation with amazing clarity long after the event is over and done with. It is like there is an image of the information deeply embossed in the mind and which can be recalled at will. The memory (in the form of an image) remains clear and sharp for a long time to come and usually is an effect that happens when some people are exposed to the same circumstance or event repeatedly.

There is no perfect understanding as to why some people can remember better without any training while others struggle to remember information even after some amount of training. However, studies have proven that repeated familiarity with the information significantly improves memory and recalling capabilities for nearly everyone.

Psychologists argue that everyone has some powers of eidetic or photographic memory; only that some of us don't have as much reel to capture and store the information as others. If scientists and experts are struggling so hard to comprehend this rather nebulous concept, then the average man is bound to have even more difficulties in that direction.

However, it is clear that people with an eidetic memory are able to remember a lot of information with a lot more accuracy than someone who does not have eidetic photographic memory. According to some experts, young children use their eidetic memory powers to help them remember things. These experts say these eidetic powers are replaced during the growth phase by verbal strategies such as rehearsing names, lists, and other details mentally.

Whatever the name used, the power of having a great memory cannot be undermined. Some classic examples of how phenomenal memory skills help some people achieve extraordinary success:

- Chess masters can play multiple opponents blindfolded; all the needed information is in their head
- Card sharks can memorize the order of a deck after it is shuffled in a couple of minutes or less

The following famous people are known to have had photographic memories, which helped them catapult to amazing success:

Nikola Tesla – This 19th-century inventor himself said that his photographic memory was one of his quirks that made him successful. He had no problem learning up entire books, and he also experienced brilliant flashes of light with hallucinating effects. Tesla admitted to having detailed visuals of his inventions much before he started tinkering with the raw materials.

Theodore Roosevelt – Known to a speed reader, Theodore Roosevelt could recite any pages of newspapers (not just the articles) as if he was reading from them. His amazing speed reading capabilities allowed him to devour 2-3 books a day.

Kim Peek – The inspiration behind the movie, Rain Man, starring Justin Hoffman, Kim Peek is believed to have memorized every word in every book he ever read (about 9000 in total). He could read each side of an open page with one eye making it possible for him to read at unprecedented speeds.

Psychiatrists who studied and analyzed Kim

Peek's abilities said that his actions proved flexibility of the human brain is far, far more than we initially thought. Like many excessively brilliant people, Kim Peek had a disability in one aspect of the brain, which seems to have been compensated with remarkable capabilities in another part.

Jerry Lucas – A top basketball player of his times (from 1962 to 1974), Lucas' other skill is his remarkable memory. He has written numerous books on memory building techniques and helped many people tips on how to make intangible and abstract information into animations and pictures with which you can make learning easy, fun, and deeply ingrained in your mind.

The good thing about memory is that you can improve it through the practice of tricks, tips, and memorization techniques, which is what this book is all about. Having a good memory helps us improve our productivity and efficiency. Just sit back, relax, and imagine a world where your memory is clear and sharp.

- You will not have to face the frustration and embarrassment of meeting someone and not being able to recall either the person's face or her name even as she exuberantly hugs you and addresses you by name as if you were her best friend
- 'I forgot' will never be an excuse in your life.
- Your best friend's or your partner's birthday card has reached him/her right on time keeping your relationship smooth and happy.
- You will know exactly where you put your glasses or your car keys and you will not waste time and energy trying to remember these mundane but important details.
- You will not have to walk into a room and wonder why you went there at all because your mind has chosen to forget the reason, thanks to your below-average recalling capabilities.
- All your passwords, PIN numbers, and other confidential data are stored safely in your head ready to be commanded at your beck and call.

Proven Benefits of Memorization Techniques

This book is full of memorization tips and tricks. How exactly do these techniques improve your memory powers? Here are some of the things that memorization techniques do for you and your brain:

They train your brain to remember – There is a memory technique that calls for you to memorize poetry. Although this exercise might seem like a waste of effort, it is an essential task that drives and trains your mind to remember things. These memory techniques exercise your brain by empowering it to retain more data than before.

They challenge your brain – Working out at the gym challenges your physical body. Memorizing techniques are the workout for your brain challenging its limits and compelling it to achieve higher levels of mental fitness. Memory techniques act as mental gymnastics exercises in improving your brain's agility and alertness.

Learning by heart improves neural plasticity – Researchers have proved that rote learning for extended periods of time helps to improve recall capacity. Repeated rote learning activates the hippocampus in the brain and improves neural plasticity enhancing the cognitive function of your brain.

Storing information for easy recall frees up your thinking power – Students who can easily recall functions, equations and definitions will be able to free up their brain power to focus on problem-solving and application-based questions. When the foundational aspects of knowledge are firmly established in the brain, you can move on to bigger and better things.

So, whether you are a student, teacher, lawyer, translator, accountant or are in any other profession, use the memory tips and techniques mentioned in this book and take your productivity and efficiency to the next level.

Chapter One:
The Human Brain and Memory

What happens in our brain when we make memories or when we try to recall them? Some people think our brain works like a computer and liken the recalling aspect to jamming a flash drive into some kind of a slot near the vicinity of your face. However, it is not that simple or convenient to understand the concept of memory storage and recall in the human brain.

You could compare your brain with Santa's sack filled with toys to be delivered at different places to different people. But, in reality, our memory is not one solid element that is stored in one place. Memory is a collection of images, conversations and ideas that are distinct from each other and need different kinds of tools for storage and recall. Moreover, the brain combines these memories in an amazingly varied number of ways to help you recover the information when you need it.

Short-Term Memory

Commonly, we think of short-term memory as being our ability to store and recall information within a short duration; typically, from a few hours to a day. However, short-term memory is, technically speaking, more fleeting than that. Short-term memory, as per scientific definition, is said to last between 15-30 seconds; akin to writing your name with a sparkler in the air. Once, the effect of the sparkler is gone, the thought is gone. Anything beyond this time is considered to be long-term memory.

If we were to use computer language, short-term memory is like the RAM – Random Access Memory that holds the data that is currently used for immediate actions and thoughts. These short-term memories can be in the form of information our senses are sending to our brain or recalling of some events or ideas that are needed for the current task you are engaged in.

Neuroscience theorizes that these short-term memory activities are performed by the neural interactions happening in the prefrontal cortex situated in front of the brain. Other aspects of short-term memory include:

- ***Limited capacity or space*** – Based on multiple observational studies, experts argue that short-term memory can hold not more than seven elements in its storage space
- ***Limited duration*** – The memory at this level is very fleeting and can easily and quickly be lost by distraction or with time
- ***Encoding*** - is primarily in the acoustic form, and even visual ideas are changed to sounds

Items in the short-term memory can be extended through repeated acoustic encoding or repeating verbally which is called rehearsing. When repeating the information is stopped, then the item is erased from the short-term memory, which is reflective of its limited duration capability. The active processes that take place in short-term memory include:

- ***Recalling information from long-term memory*** – For example, if you need to fill your father's name in on an application form, the process in your short-term memory will retrieve this data from the long-term memory.
- ***Rehearsing data*** – As discussed above, if you need to keep the information in your short-term memory for a longer duration than its current capability, then you would have to rehearse it through verbal encoding
- ***Selective attention to sensory memory*** – For example, if you are sitting on a chair, you will not remember the pressure of the sitting position on your bottom unless you focus your attention on the sense.

Moreover, as scientific research developed on human memory, the concept of short-term memory has taken on a new name and additional aspects. It is referred to as working memory and includes the following aspects too:

- The fact that short-term memory has different processes could mean that there are different

areas for these functions
- People with damaged brains lose memory selectively while some other elements function normally suggesting that memory span, rehearsing, re-coding and transferring data to long-term memory use different parts of the brain system, and these are independent of each other
- Although at the basic level, short-term memory does not seem to be connected to reading, reasoning, verbal processing or other such types of complex intelligence elements, studies have shown that, at a more complex level, these aspects of memory and intelligence take place at the short-term memory span too

Long-Term Memory

In this place, the memory becomes a 'physical thing.' If short-term memory can be likened to your computer's RAM, then long-term memory can be likened to its hard-drive where everything in your life is stored. Long-term memory has a physical presence in the brain and is not only dependent on any kind of specific neural activity.

In long-term memory, neurons connect with each other physically through synapses that endure whether they are used or not. Remember, in the short-term memory, if the data is not used, it is out of that space? Long-term memory is the opposite; even if you don't use the data, it remains in that space. Long-term memory can be further split into two types; implicit memory and explicit memory

Implicit Memory – deals with skills and habits that are done automatically and without thought. Examples of activities handled by implicit memory include driving a car, rolling a cigarette, swinging a bat, typing on the keyboard, humming an old and familiar tune, or any kind of habits that you have developed. This kind of memory is unconscious and unintentional.

Recalling from implicit memory happens without your conscious knowledge. You don't have to stop and think how to roll a cigarette or swing a bat. Riding a bicycle is a classic example of implicit memory. If you have to ride a bike for the first time after a long gap, then too, you will be able to hop on to a cycle and ride effortlessly.

Explicit Memory – deals with ideas that you intentionally try to remember and are conscious of the efforts that go into making memories and recalling them. For example, trying to remember a scientific formula for your exam is an example of using your explicit memory. We use our explicit memory every day; from trying to recall the time of the doctor's appointment or studying for a test, etc. Also referred to as declarative memory, this kind of memory requires you conscious and explicit efforts to remember and recall.

Examples of explicit memory include learning for a test or trying to remember what was taught in your physics class, recalling the phone number of your friend or that incident in high school that happened a few years ago or the capital of France or the current US President, etc. Explicit memory can be further divided into two types; episodic memory and semantic memory.

Episodic memory involves episodes and events that happened to you such as what happened during your high school or college or in your love life. *Semantic memory* involves general data and information such as the capital of France or the name of the US President.

An illustration to discern between episodic and semantic memory is as follows: recalling the fact that Paris is the capital of France is a semantic memory; recalling how you fell ill on your Paris trip last year is an episodic memory.

Encoding and Consolidation

Encoding is a complex process that weaves through millions of neurons and neural activity that help in memorizing things in such a way that you can recall them later on. When we actually make an effort to remember something, then it's the long-term memory that we concerned about.

So, how do long-term memories form? The first step in creating long-term memories is to encode the information quickly failing which it will be lost just like breath on a mirror or the writing of your name in the air with a sparkler.

Several parts of the brain play a part in the process of encoding and consolidating information. The most important parts of the brain involved in this process are the hippocampus, the amygdala, and the cerebellum. Let us look at each of them in a bit of detail for better understanding:

The hippocampus – is that region of the brain that is responsible for forming new memories. It is also that place in the brain in which new neurons are generated regularly. The hippocampus connects and bonds all the new events and data and forms synaptic connections and encodes them into a new memory. A good analogy is someone knitting a rich and complex tapestry in real-time.

However, the hippocampus does not treat all information equally. The things that are 'important' get preference over things that are not so critical. For example, the hippocampus will prioritize those memories that have a strong emotional bond (maybe the date and amount of your salary) for you than something more routine or incomprehensible such as your daily commute to office or the lyrics of a foreign language song.

The hippocampus is very selective in its approach to encoding new memories because it is always very busy, and prioritizing is the only way it can function effectively. After the information is encoded and consolidated, it ceases to be in the hippocampus. Studies have revealed that the hippocampus does not play a crucial role in memory retention after the consolidation process.

Any damage to the hippocampus results in difficulties in the realm of making new memories. However, some studies revealed that these people can recall older memories because as new memories are formed, the neuron synapses that represent older memories seem to get pushed further into the cortex.

The amygdala – is known to be involved in memory consolidation, or more specifically, modulation, which is the intensity with which the memory is stored in the brain. Specifically, it is noted that the arousal of emotion after a particular incident enhances the depth of consolidation of the memory. The greater the emotional arousal, the stronger the memory consolidation. However, even if the amygdala is damaged, encoded memories can be recalled.

The cerebellum – is known to be responsible for learning structured and procedural memory such as routine and practiced skills and motor skills such as playing a musical instrument, riding a cycle, or driving a car. Damage to the cerebellum can result in the loss of motor and coordination control.

So, a person with damage in his hippocampus

might be able to recall how to play the piano will not be able to recall other facts of his life. And, a person with a damaged cerebellum might be able to recall old facts from his life but may have forgotten to play the piano, as earlier.

Similar kinds of memories tend to clump together; visual memories close to the visual cortex, spoken memories close to the language centers, etc. Moreover, there is an accumulation of redundancy where you could have the same memory stored in different ways. Each time you activate these memories, they get stronger than before. Memories are not stored like books in a library; they are continuously tweaked and updated.

Memory and Emotions

The various memory-based studies have found one very intriguing aspect that influences our brain's ability to remember and recall information; our emotional state at the time our brain received this information. Emotions are also known to help in retrieving the data when we revisit it. Putting ourselves in the same frame of mind as it was when the event happened is believed to make recalling easy.

Studies have proven that emotionally charged memories last longer and are easier to recall than those memories, which have no emotional, connect. When we feel anger, happiness, or delight, then we have a more vivid recollections of what happened than the routine everyday tasks that have little or no emotional connection for us.

For example, you can recall the events of your first date that happened many years ago more vividly than the scene of filling your cat's dinner bowl with food just yesterday or how many beers you had last Saturday or what color socks you wore to the office yesterday. Our brains can retain and retrieve those memories that are emotionally charged. In addition to emotions, other aspects that affect our memory include moods and attention.

Recalling Memories from the Recesses of the Brain

So, how can we recall specific bits of information from the big chunk of data that is scattered all over the brain? It might look like the so-called old memories have turned to dust because you have forgotten a lot of things such as old passwords, addresses, deadlines, etc. What you must remember is that you haven't forgotten them; your recalling ability has simply become reduced in intensity. It's like a glove that you have forgotten where you put. You still own the glove; you simply don't know where you have put it.

Recalling memories is a mysterious brain function, and how information from the dark recesses of our brain is accessed is a work-in-progress project for neuroscientists. It is uncertain how our frontal cortex of the brain accesses the stored information and makes it relevant for use in the present. However, it is quite certain that the more you use this capability, the easier it is to find the data.

Therefore, it makes sense to work on and perfect a few memory improvement techniques to keep our brains active, and also to leverage the benefits of a more productive and meaningful life.

Chapter Two: Creative Thinking and Visualization for Memory

How does creative thinking and visualization help in improving your memory? Many studies have revealed that visualization and creative thinking are directly connected to memory. When we try to remember things from our past, we access our episodic memory, which, in turn, helps in triggering creative, divergent thinking.

Episodic memory helps us to time travel mentally into the past as well as the future thereby building our creativity while improving our memory. Essentially, when we delve deep into detailed aspects of our past or into the dreams for our future, our brain is primed to think creatively.

In the same way, our brain is able to remember

better through visualization and creative thinking techniques because humans can remember images better than written or verbal information. For example, if you have shifted homes, you will notice that you can clearly remember the design and details of the living room and bedrooms in each house. However, you may not be able to recall street names, door numbers, or telephone numbers with the same vividness.

Images are concrete and tangible whereas raw information in the form of written or spoken words is quite abstract making it more difficult to store and recall the latter format. However, it is possible to convert these abstract elements into tangible forms through memory techniques based on visualization and creative thinking.

These images become your mental hooks using which you can retrieve information from your long-term memory archives. While one of the primary reasons visualization techniques for memory work is that our brain remembers images well, there are other reasons too.

Visualization techniques help to improve other aspects of memory including repetition and concentration.

So, if you have problems with concentration, visualization techniques are great remedies to get better at it. When you use visualization methods to remember some things, you are compelled to keep your focus on that process; effectually, you have no choice but to focus on your task. Creating mental images is a powerful focusing exercise. Additionally, as you keep exposing your mind repeatedly on the item for which you are creating visual images, the repetitive aspect of memorization is exercised.

Repetition is a key element for memorization. For example, if you meet someone for the first time, and she mentions her name only once, you are quite likely to forget the name. However, during the conversation, if the individual repeats her name more than once, it is quite likely you will not forget it. However, people don't really help us out like this, do they?

Creating mental images makes you repeat each detail of the memory you are making, again and again, to ensure each image is crystal clear and easily recallable when you need it. Therefore, creative thinking and visualization techniques help you increase your memory powers because of the following reasons:

- The human brain finds it easier to remember concrete, tangible images rather than intangible, vague written or spoken words
- Creating images improves your focusing capability; an important aspect of memory skills
- Continuous review of the images will help to reinforce the original memory repeatedly thereby improving memory skills

Moreover, visualization techniques are not difficult to turn into habit. Initially, it might take some time to create images for everything. However, as you practice each day, you will find it increasingly easy to associate memories with images. You will be able to do it almost unconsciously with sufficient practice.

Remembering Types of Volcanoes

Here are some examples of connecting images with complex names. Suppose you need to remember the shape of each type of volcano.

There are three types of volcanoes including cinder cones, shield volcanoes, and stratovolcanoes. Now, your job is to remember the shape of stratovolcanoes so that you can recall it whenever when you need to. Cinder cones form quickly and are small structures consisting of ash and cinders. Shield volcanoes are flat and wide, like a shield, and stratovolcanoes are very high with a pointed peak.

- Cinder volcanoes – cinder and small
- Shield volcanoes – flat and wide (like a shield)
- Stratovolcanoes – high and pointed (like a hill)

Examples of stratovolcanoes include Mount Fiji and Mount Ranier. Now, how can you remember strato and connect it to the 'high and pointed?'

Well, here is a tip. Strato sounds like 'straight-O,' and you can imagine a line of O's marching up the pointed-peaked tall high in a straight line.

This image you have created will help you connect stratovolcanoes with 'high and pointed' helping you recognize the picture anywhere you see it. The clearer the image of the memory in your head, the easier it will be to recall. Moreover, the sillier, larger, and more imaginative the picture is, the easier to remember and recall.

More pictures and word-connections

Here are some wild ways of creating images with simple words that illustrate the wild aspect of visualization techniques and improved memory. You can use similar techniques to remember big and complex words:

Charts – Divide this word as char + 'tz' (sounds similar). Char means something burned and black, and 'tz' sounds like the letter zee. So, to remember the word 'charts' you could visualize a huge Z which is completely black and charred.

Source – Source sounds like sour + sea; so how about a lemon-filled ocean?

Data – Data pronounced loosely sounds like 'day' + 'tie.' So, an image of the sun (it is out during the day) trying hard to wear a tie can help you remember the word day + tie which, in turn, because of the association in your mind, you will be able to recall the word, 'data.'

So, like this, you must try and connect complex words with images, which will create a mental hook connecting the word, and the image in your mind making it easy to remember and recall. It might appear bizarre initially for the novice. It is this 'wild' perception that actually creates the right hooking system for excellent recall later on.

Moreover, these visualization techniques are used by performers to achieve superhuman capabilities. If you can achieve even a fraction of that success, your productivity levels will improve significantly.

Chapter Three: Peg System Memory Techniques

The peg system helps you to remember lists of things like school work, to-do-lists, and other order-based tasks very easily. The peg system also creates an ordered filing format in your brain making it easier to retrieve the required data when needed.

The peg system connects new information by associating it with old data that is already deeply embedded in your mind. Such old data which is used for pegging new data could be the alphabets from A to Z or numbers from 1 to 20, etc. A peg is like a mental hook where you hang the information onto the old information so that you can access it easily.

For example, look at the numbers 1 to 10. If you

associate an important memory item with number five, then all you need to do is remember number 5, and your brain will recall the associated item. Before we go into peg system techniques, here are some important elements:

It helps you remember the new data – Unlike rote learning where you simply mug up the data and hope to remember the order correctly, the peg system will connect what you know very well, and help you recall what you need which is the new data. It acts like a loci system by being in the center of all the important things in your life and connecting them to the new data as and when they are added.

It allows you to retrieve information from memory directly – Using the peg system, you can run through the items using the old data, and pick out the one you need directly. You simply run through the entire link until you get to the item that is needed immediately. For example, if you are talking about the list of nerves in the cranial system, and you know the fifth one is the trigeminal nerve, then #5 is connected to it, which becomes your peg system.

You can reuse the peg systems repeatedly – An amazing thing about our brain is that it can associate the same peg system to remember a multitude of information. So, you can connect numbers 1-10 to the set of cranial nerves or the geometrical shapes with varying sides, and your brain will connect the number 5 to the trigeminal nerves when you are thinking about biology and will connect it to a pentagon when you are dealing with geometry. Therefore, the same peg system can be used repeatedly to remember many kinds of information.

You can use any kind of peg system for added flexibility – For example, you can use the even numbers (2, 4, 6, 8...) to remember something, and use odd numbers (1, 3, 5, 7...) for others. This way, you can add flexibility, and also have something unique to remember each type of information as well.

How Does the Peg System Work

It is impossible for an average human being to forget numbers and alphabets, right? Peg systems connect new data to these unforgettable lists to help you remember and recall. However, the problem with numbers and alphabets is that they are abstract forms of data; they are not concrete or tangible objects, and therefore difficult to remember if used directly. The peg system allows you to give tangible forms and shapes to this kind of abstract data.

For example, using rhyming peg words, you can connect numbers to tangible objects such as One-sun, two-shoe, three-tree, and more. To recall the list, simply run through the numbers connect the object to the numbers and find what you are looking for. Then, to remember a list by connecting it to the objects you have given to your peg system. Let us look at a few peg systems for illustration purposes:

The Number-Rhyme Peg System

For each of the numbers from 1-10, find the name of an object that you can easily relate to. The following list is a commonly used peg system number:

- One – sun, bun, gun
- Two – Shoe, zoo, glue
- Three – tree, sea, bee
- Four – door, store
- Five – hive, wife, knife
- Six – sticks, pigs, bricks
- Seven – heaven,
- Eight – gate, plate, skate
- Nine – vine, sign, mine, wine
- Ten – hen, pen

Now, suppose you need to remember the following list; egg, motorbike, plate, shirt, book, coconut, mobile phone, ice cream, mirror, and umbrella. Here are some tips to create a peg system for this list:

- You are frying an egg with the sun's rays streaming into the kitchen – the sun is connected to the first item on the list viz. the egg
- The motorbike runs over your pretty shoes squashing them and rendering them useless – the second list item on the list is connected to the shoe
- Plates are hanging from the tree and are banging against each other as the branches are swaying wildly in the wind – the 3rd item, plate, is connected to tree
- You are covering the gap between the door and the floor to prevent buzzing mosquitoes from entering your house – 4th item connected to door
- A huge bloody knife is stuck out of your Math book because you are so angry that you cannot remember the formulae – 5th item and knife
- You are flinging coconuts on the pigs that disturb you with their grunting while you sleep – 6th item coconut connected to pigs

- The angel from heaven is calling you on your mobile phone – 7th item, mobile phone, is linked through the imagery to heaven
- An ice-cream cone is stuck on your gate because you don't want your mother to know you are eating it – 8th item – ice-cream connected to gate
- A madman is using red wine to clean his mirror, and all the reflections in the mirror are also appearing red – 9th item connected to wine
- A big fat hen is running around in the farm with an umbrella stuck in her feathers as it doesn't want to get wet – 10th item connected to hem

Now, can you recall the seventh item? Well, seven, heaven, angel calling your mobile phone; therefore the seventh item is mobile phone! Try this exercise randomly, and you will notice you are getting better with each attempt. Tips for numbers 11-20:

- Eleven – Leaven,
- Twelve – Elf, Shelf

- Thirteen – thirsting, hurting
- Fourteen – courting, fording
- Fifteen – lifting, fitting
- Sixteen – licking, Sistine
- Seventeen – deafening, leavening
- Eighteen – waiting, aiding
- Nineteen – pining, knighting
- Twenty – Plenty, penny (to rhyme with the slang way of saying twenny)

The Number-Shape Peg System

This is similar to the number-rhyme peg system except that you use the shape of the number to connect. For numbers 1-10, the connections will be something like this:

- 1 – shape of a stick
- 2 – shape of a duck or swan floating in water
- 3 – The top part of the heart-shape
- 4 – shape of a boat with its sails unfurled
- 5 – the shape of a hook
- 6 – shape of a golf stick
- 7 – the shape of the edge of a cliff

- 8 – shape of an hourglass
- 9 – shape of a balloon at the end of a stick
- 10 – figure of a fork and a plate kept next to each other

Now, suppose you have to remember a list in which the second item is a tomato. So, here is what you can imagine; a tomato dancing on the back of a beautiful white swan on a clear blue lake. So, the connection here is the swan, which is the shape of #2. You can form your own visuals using the techniques given in the Number-Rhyme peg system (of the tomato example) for the rest of the names in the list you need to remember.

Alphabet Peg System

You already know the alphabets and so can recall them with ease, and therefore, they can be used as an excellent memory pegging system. Typically, there are two ways you can use the alphabet peg system; one is using the concrete meaning of the word you associate the alphabet with, and two, based on sound-alike words.

Here are the alphabets followed by 1) the concrete meaning associated with the alphabet, and 2) the rhyming or similar-sounding word:

- A – Alligator, Hay
- B – Boy, Bee
- C – Cat, See
- D – Dog, Dead
- E – Egg, Eve
- F – Fig, Effort
- G – Goat, Jeep
- H – Hat, Age
- I – Ice, Eye
- J – Jack, Jay
- K – Kite, Key
- L – Log, Ell
- M – Man, Hem
- N – Nut, Hen
- O – Owl, Hoe
- P – Pig, Pea
- Q – Quill, Cue
- R – Rock, Oar
- S – Sock, Sass
- T – Toy, Tea

- U – Umbrella, Ewe
- V – Vane, Veal
- W – Wig, Double you
- X - X-Ray, Axe
- Y – Yak, Wire
- Z – Zoo, Zebra

So, to memorize a list of 26 items using the sound-alike alphabet system, you can imagine the first item to be in the midst, the second one being stung by a bee, and so forth. You can use similar imaging techniques to peg your lists to the items connected to the concrete objects linked to each alphabet.

Like all memory techniques, the peg system is also a skill that gets better with practice and sustained effort. Additionally, if you notice the illustrative examples given to use the peg system, there are plenty of visuals and creative thinking that went into making up the images. So, by combining your visualization techniques and the peg system, you can learn to remember anything you want to remember with ease.

Chapter Four:
Tips to Remember Names

People relationships are a key element to personal and professional success. Whether you are a student, student, teacher, lawyer, translator, accountant, or the CEO of an organization, knowing and recalling people's names can improve the success in your particular field. When you remember someone's name, it tells the person that he or she is important to you, and there is a sense of obligation created to reciprocate this feeling. So, here are some great tips to remember people's names.

Know Your Motivation for Remembering the Concerned Individual's Name

Motivation drives memory. If you don't understand and appreciate the importance of your need to remember a person's name, you will forget it. Imagine this person is carrying a bag with $100,000 in it for your cause. Will you forget this person's name? Of course, you will not. You will delve deep into the recesses of your brain, and use every memory technique to recall his name. Reason for remembering reaps results.

Focus on the Conversation

You will not remember the person you spoke to if you are daydreaming or are distracted during the conversation. Make sure you focus on the conversation and actively participate in it. The primary reason for not remembering people's names is you are not listening. And this is not an issue of memory but mere lack of focus.

The details of any task will not embed in your memory if you are not paying attention. The same holds good for conversations too. Pay attention so that the details of what transpired between the two (including the person's name) get registered in the brain.

Focusing on the conversation includes not being

distracted by your internal thoughts. You might be quiet on the outside. But, on the inside (in your mind), a lot of thoughts are going on. Especially, in a panic situation, you end up so worried that you will never remember the person's name at the right time that you could miss out the place where his or her name was mentioned. Focus your entire body and mind on the conversations and don't let thoughts wander off somewhere.

Repeat the Person's Name

Repetition is a powerful memory tool and can be easily used during conversations to remember people's name. For example, if you are introduced to someone called, you can always shake his hand and say, "Pleased to meet you, John," or "Nice to meet you, John." That's the only undeniable opportunity you will get to repeat a person's name.

However, for this tip to be successful, you must focus and pay attention when the person's name was mentioned to you. Conversely, if you get into the habit of repeating people's names during the conversation, you will be forced to focus. So, this tip will help you with both tips.

Another way to repeat the person's name is to use his or her name is to find other opportunities to say it, definitely when you are saying goodbye. Practice makes perfect. You can recollect how this newly met person reminds you of another person who is already in your social circle.

See If You Can Find Something Unique in the Person's Face

Look out for a distinctive feature about the person's face. Perhaps, an unusual nose, the color of his or her eyes, a different hairstyle, large ears, or anything else that seems to stand out for you. Typically, the most outstanding feature you notice the first time you meet someone is the one that you can remember easily later on. Connecting the person's name to the visual feature is a creative visualization technique that you already know to be an effective memory tactic.

Connect the Person's Name with Something You Already Know

Even for a common name like John, you can have something that is important to you to which you can connect and recall easily. For example, if you are an avid Bible reader, you can connect John to John the Baptist or the Gospel of John. If you are an avid follower of politics, you can connect your John to John F. Kennedy. If you love music, link John to John Lennon, and so forth. This connection with someone or something that is close to your heart can help you remember names easily.

Use Visualization Techniques

For example, if the person's (who has curly hair) name is Mr. Bender, imagine him bending over a water tank and getting his curls all wet. If his name is Mr. Baldwin, then imagine a bald man on a winning streak in a poker game. The wilder and crazier the image, the easier it is to remember the person's name. Here are more examples which you can extrapolate as you wish:

- Steve – think of a stove over which he is cooking your favorite dish
- Paul – think of a 'ball' in your favorite game
- Hamilton – think of a ton of ham balancing precariously on his nose
- Dave – connect it to your daily shave
- Margaret – imagine margarine melting down her blonde hair

Make a List of the Names of New People You Met During the Day

At the end of the day, make a note of the names of the people you met on that day, either mentally or a physical list. It might seem like a wasted effort initially, but these small acts are what drive your brain to remember things. When you make an effort to crystallize your thoughts, your brain will find it easier to store it in a place from where you can retrieve the information when you need it later on.

And finally, even before you go on to read the tips on how to remember names, the first step is to commit to yourself that you are going to walk down this path of remembering names. It has to be a commitment from your end to find ways to remember people's names. For example, you cannot use the excuse of a 'bad memory' for not being able to remember and recall names. You have to work at it, and you have to give yourself this commitment.

Moreover, remembering people's name improves people management skills endearing you to the people who are important to you helping you achieve success in your professional and personal relationships.

Chapter Five:
Mind Mapping Tips

Mind mapping is a powerful tool to capture your thoughts and give them tangibility. Mind maps are a visual tool that can be used to improve all cognitive functions including learning, analysis, memory and creativity. Mind mapping follows a combination of images, color and visual-spacing aspects to write down and structure information in your brain in such a way that recalling and remembering will become significantly easier.

Instead of simply taking down notes, creating mind maps will help you improve your creativity, remember things clearly, and improve your problem-solving abilities.

What are Mind Maps?

A mind map is a diagrammatic representation of a central idea or theme, which is surrounded by connected information about the central theme. So, for example, if your central idea is poetry, then that takes the center place, and all the connected ideas are placed in a radial structure around it.

The radial branches emerging from the central root idea of poetry are typically the subtopics of the primary topic. So, your subtopics for poetry could include:

- Types of poetry
- Famous poets
- Famous works
- Important publications

Each of these branching out subtopics will have branches of its own. For example, the branch of 'types of poetry' will include sub-branches such as classical poetry, contemporary poetry, etc. Each level of branches get more and more detailed and, finally, they can all be linked together.

Mind maps can be used for a variety of learning,

thinking and memory tasks from learning a new subject to planning a career to building better habits, to making your memory more powerful than before. Here are the steps to create a mind map:

Step 1 – Create a Central Concept

The central concept is the beginning point of your mind map, which is the main topic you are going to follow. It should be placed in the middle of your mind map page. An accompanying image of the central topic will enhance the encoding process in your brain making it easier to remember and recall. It is important to take time and effort to personalize your central idea. This customized approach will help in connecting with the other content on the page easier than otherwise.

Step 2 – Now, Build Branches to Your Central Theme

The next logical step to the building of a mind map is to create main branches around your main concept. The main branches are the most important sub-themes associated with the central idea. You can add child branches to each of the main sub-themes to achieve greater depth in your learning.

This ability to keep adding child branches is one of the most attractive aspects of mind mapping. You can keep adding new data over the existing data with each new addition enhancing your knowledge associated with the previous ones. The structure of the mind map will flow as naturally as your thoughts develop. The fluidity that mind mapping offers makes the learning process fun and engaging giving you the flexibility to go as deep as you wish.

Step 3 – Include Keywords

Each time a new branch is added, a new idea should be represented using one word only. The importance of limiting the keyword for each idea is one that cannot be underestimated. With one word to describe an idea, a plethora of associated ideas will flow limitlessly as against using a string of words or a phrase.

For example, if you use the words 'birthday party,' you will be restricted to only those aspects associated with birthday party such as venue, time, date, etc. However, if your idea was represented by only with 'birthday,' then your repertoire of ideas will be more extensive, and you can include cake, invitees, presents, etc.

Moreover, keeping one word per branch will help you chunk all the information regarding that one word under one heading resulting in a more compact mind map. Using keywords also triggers brain connections resulting in improved memory and recall ability.

Step 4 – Color Code Your Branches

Mind mapping involves your entire brain to participate in the learning and memory-retentive process because it combines a broad array of cortical skills ranging from logical to numerical to creativity and more.

When all these cognitive powers overlap and intertwine with each other, your brain functioning becomes more synergetic resulting in optimal output. It is not good to isolate different types of cortical functions as brain development is compromised significantly.

Another way to increase cortical overlap is to color code the branches on your mind map. Color coding helps your brain by connecting the visual skills to the logical, numerical and creative parts helping in the creation of shortcuts. These mental shortcuts in your brain will help you retain the information from the mind map in a clear way and facilitating easy recall.

Additionally, colors enhance the appealing and attractive aspect of your mind map helping you to continuously engage with it as you keep adding more branches as your learning progresses.

Step 5 – Include As Many Images As You Can

By now you know the power of images and your

brain's capability to recall images better than the spoken or the written word. Images can convey an entire story and far more information than a whole page of text. Images are processed immediately by our brains and also are visual stimuli for memory recall. Also, images speak a universal language that has the power to cross all linguistic barriers. To leverage these powers of using images, ensure your mind map is covered with as many images as you can put.

Mind maps are excellent memory and learning tools and help you in the following ways:

- They help you remember and recall information of all kinds
- They make you think of all possible connections and drive you to have a brainstorming session with yourself
- They help you stay organized
- They help you see all the connections and links of the primary idea
- They save you time by allowing you to learn using only single words instead of entire

sentences
- They fit into only one side of the paper thereby saving you space and keeping all related information in a compact manner
- They help you see the project in its entirety as well as its smaller working parts that seamlessly connect with one another
- They help you add new ideas and thoughts without having to rewrite the entire project

Chapter Six:
Memory Palace

Used since the time of the ancient Romans, the Memory Palace is one of the most powerful memory tools that are not only easy to learn but engaging and fun too. It is an extremely useful technique to learn and master to improve your productivity and efficiency irrespective of whether you are a student, lawyer, accountant, or in any other profession.

The principle of the Memory Palace technique is based on the fact that the human brain can easily recollect and remember places that we know. This 'memory palace' is nothing but a favorite location of yours that you recall with ease. This palace can be a room inside your home or your commuting route or any other familiar place that is deeply etched in your mind. The familiarity of the place will act as your guide even as you store information and recall it when needed. Here are some important steps to follow to create your Memory Palace:

Step 1 – Choose Your Memory Palace

The most important thing to bear in mind while choosing your palace is your familiarity with the place. The effectiveness of this technique is entirely dependent on how easy it is for you to wander around your palace and see things clearly in your mind.

Your palace should be a place where you can be present (yes, mentally) at will, anywhere, anytime. The more clearly and vividly you can recall the intricate details of your palace, the more effective this technique will be. An effective first choice is your own home.

You must also create a walking path in your mind palace that is constantly moving around in the way you want it to. The palace should not be a static one; instead, it should be a dynamic one that your mind's eye can travel through with ease.

Therefore, instead of simply focusing on the static outside façade of your home, take a visual trip. For example, watch the emergence of the various places in your home as you walk in through the front door; pass the living room into the corridor that leads into the bedroom even as you catch sight of the dining room to your left. A specific order of the path will also improve the effectiveness of this technique.

Here are some more tips on the kind of memory palace you can choose:

- Possible routes to your workplace.
- Any street in your city that you are familiar with
- Your high school or college – Here you can imagine the various paths leading to your classrooms, the library, the basketball court, and other places that you enjoy being in
- Your office – Imagine the door opening into the main building of your office. Imagine walking down the familiar path to your cabin, saying hi to the different people seated at

their desks, and other such scenes
- A park in your neighborhood

Step 2 – Make a List of Distinctive Features

The next step is to pay attention to the various features in your memory palace. For example, if you have chosen your home as your memory palace, then the front door will be the first distinctive feature. Then walk into your house and make a mental note of all the things you can see which could include:

- That picture on the wall
- The dining table
- The open kitchen and its various cabinets

Each of these features will become a memory slot in your palace.

Step 3 – Imprint Your Memory Palace in Your Head

You have to be able to commit to memory all the distinctive features of this memory palace entirely in your mind. There has to be an image deeply imprinted in your head. If visual learning is your strength, then this might not be very difficult for you. For the others, here are a few tips:

- Literally walk through your memory palace (physically, not mentally) and say out loud all the distinctive features along the path
- Next, make a written note of these features, and commit them to memory even as you mentally walk through the memory palace
- Make sure you see the distinctive feature from the same perspective
- When you think your imprint is thorough, repeat it again and again until there is not an iota of doubt

When this imprint of your memory palace is stamped on your mind, you are ready to use it. You can reuse this palace any number of times to remember anything you want to.

Step 4 – Create Associations

Now, that you have deeply entrenched in your

mind, create associations for each of the things you need to remember using the tips given in the Peg System (Chapter 3). Each memory peg will be one distinctive feature in your memory palace. Here is an example to illustrate how this works. Suppose we need to make a grocery list with your memory palace. Suppose the list you have in mind is as follows:

- Bacon
- Eggs
- Flour

There are only three items for illustrative purposes. You can use any number of items into your list and remember them with ease. Now, the first three distinctive features in your home memory place are the front door, the picture on the wall, and the dining table. Now, associate the above items as follows:

- Bacon – imagine a huge piece of bacon stuck on your front door and the neighbors are laughing at the scene
- Eggs – Imagine eggs being thrown on that

picture on the wall and the gooey insides trickling down the picture
- Floor – Imagine flour being dusted all over your dining table

Now, at the grocer's, when you need to recall these items, walk mentally through your memory palace and recall these vivid associations and the grocery list will come in a flash.

Step 5 – Keep Visiting Your Palace

If you are new to this concept, you might need to have a few rehearsals for the initial memory exercise. Therefore, keep visiting your palace, and keep making mental notes of the distinctive features. As your palace grows, the number of these features will also grow. As you complete one tour of your palace, turn around, and walk in the reverse direction until you reach the starting point of your palace.

The Memory Palace is an effective visual and creative thinking-based memory tool that will never go out of fashion for you because you are dealing with something tangible that you are very familiar with. Moreover, as you keep using your Memory Palace, the familiarity is going to increase enhancing the effectiveness of this memory improvement technique.

Chapter Seven: General Tips for Improved Memory

While visual techniques, mind map techniques, peg systems and memory palaces are specific methods to improve your memory capabilities; there are general health-based and mental exercises that boost your memory. Let us look at some of them in this chapter.

Powerful Memory-Boosting Mental Exercises

Mental activities help your brain to move away from its familiar path of thinking and set up new neural connections thereby improving its functioning and skills. Sticking to the same path of thinking will result in your brain becoming inactive and dull. You have to keep challenging it to new levels and planes of thought.

Memory is like muscle power; if you don't use it, you lose it. Here are many more benefits of indulging in powerful memory-boosting mental exercises:

It teaches you new ways of thinking – Irrespective of how mentally challenging your work is, your brain achieves a sense of familiarity, and cognitive strength will begin to stagnate instead of developing more. The way to break its familiar way of thinking is to make the brain do unfamiliar mental activities, and that is what different kinds of mental exercise will achieve for you.

It challenges your brain – Brain-boosting exercises require you to give your complete attention and focus. For example, playing a musical piece (no matter how hard) that you already know well is not challenging to the brain. However, learning to play a new song (no matter how seemingly easy) challenges your brain to achieve higher levels of thinking and memory skills.

Choose mental activities and games that take you from an easy level slowly to more difficult ones. That way, each time your brain is challenged to do things better than the previous level.

Here are some brain-boosting exercises that you can indulge in as often as you can:

Recalling Self-Tests - Make a list of things you need to do such as a grocery list or to-do list or the names of people in your high school or anything else. Now, arrange them in an order, and use any of the techniques to learn up the list by heart. Now, take a break for an hour, and then try and recall what you have learned. Repeat this exercise as often as you can to improve your memory powers.

Learn to play an instrument or to sing – Music is known to have immense memory-boosting capabilities. Learning music either in the vocal form or playing an instrument is known to improve memory capabilities significantly. Multiple studies connect memory to music.

Sometimes, even listening to your favorite music can help in the learning process. However, when you are studying, it is better to listen only to instrumental as lyrics of a song can be quite a distraction.

Do some complex math in your head – Take two 3-digit numbers and try to add them in your head without the help of a calculator or even a paper and pencil. Make it more difficult by indulging in a physical exercise while doing the arithmetic problem. You could choose to increase the intensity of the math problem by multiplying instead of adding.

Learn to cook – Cooking involves the use of multiple sensory organs including touch, smell, sight, and taste. Each of these sensory organs involves the working of different parts of the brain, which is great for optimal brain functioning.

Learn a new language – A new language which involves hearing and talking new words stimulate the brain increasing its functioning and your memory skills.

Indulge in a hobby involving hand-eye coordination – Knitting, painting, assembling a puzzle, drawing, etc. are hobbies that involve hand-eye coordination, which improves brain functioning.

Lifestyle-Related Memory-Boosting Tips

Get Sufficient Sleep

This is the easiest and effective way to boost your memory. After you have learned something new, take a short nap or get a good night's restful sleep. Multiple studies have proven that people who sleep over a new idea or lesson are able to remember much better than those who did not get sleep after the lesson. Sleep is an important phase when the brain is able to not only embed the memories deep within its recesses but also in a way that makes retrieval easy for you.

Sleep resets our brain (much like the save button

on your computer applications), and therefore, critical for memory and learning. If you don't enough sleep, the neurons in your brain get overactive with electrical impulses buzzing around crazily making it difficult to register and encode new memories. Sleep is mandatory for the memory consolidation process.

Therefore, late-night cramming before an exam should be avoided as much as possible. Instead, regular study and sufficient sleep work wonders to help you clear exams with flying colors. Researchers also opine that a 45-60 minute nap after learning something new will help in retention and recall by nearly 500%.

Another important aspect of sleep is to know the difference between the amount of sleep you need to get on and the amount you need for optimal functioning of your entire body system including your brain. Here are some important pointers about sleep:

Get a regular sleep schedule – Keep your bedtime and wake-up time constant as much as possible. Avoid breaking your sleep schedule even on holidays and weekends.

Switch off all your electronic screens at least one hour before your bedtime – The blue light that emits from tablets, phones, TVs, and computers make you feel wakeful as it suppresses the production of sleep-inducing hormones such as melatonin.

Exercise

Sleep is one pillar of brain strength. Physical exercise is another important pillar. Our brains need a continuous supply of oxygen-rich blood for optimal functioning. And what better way to ensure this continuous supply than a good amount of physical exercise? Exercise is the best and the most effective way to drive blood to the brain and improve its functioning.

Physical exercise such as running and jogging triggers the increased production and release of a protein called cathepsin B. This protein, in turn, is responsible for increased neuron growth in the hippocampus area of the brain resulting in new memory connections. Other studies have proven that waiting for about 4 hours after learning a new lesson will help in improved retention and recall capabilities. Here are some brain-boosting tips for your exercise regimen:

- Aerobic exercise is great for your brain as it keeps your blood pumping. Generally, anything that is good for the heart is good for the brain
- If you take a long time to clear out your sleep fog, then exercising in the morning is the best. It not only clears your sleep fog well but also primes your mind for improved learning throughout the day.
- Physical activities with complex motor skills or hand-eye coordination are particularly good for improving brain functioning
- Exercise breaks during the day help clear mental fatigue, especially the post-lunch slump. A short walk is sufficient for brain reboot

Eat Healthily

Trans-fats and saturated fats from red meats are connected to bad memory. Researchers have concluded from various studies that cholesterol can clog your heart as well as your brain. The plaques from cholesterol buildup can lead to damage of brain tissues resulting in a reduced supply of oxygen-rich blood thereby impairing learning and memory.

On the contrary, unsaturated fat-rich diets (typically fruit and veggies, seafood, nuts, olive oil, etc.) are connected to improved memory and cognitive skills. Here are some more diet-based ideas for improved memory:

Get your omega-3 fatty acids – fish is particularly rich in omega-3 fatty acids (which are linked strongly to memory boosting powers). Include a lot of fish such as salmon, mackerel, halibut, tuna, and more 'fatty' fish. Other sources of omega-3 fatty acids include walnuts, seaweed, flaxseed and its oil, pinto and kidney beans, winter squash, etc.

Include a lot of fruit and vegetables – They are full of antioxidants that protect your brain cells from damage. The more colorful the fruit and vegetables are, the richer in antioxidants they are.

Avoid caffeine – Caffeine affects different people in different ways. For some of us, even the morning coffee could have an effect on the night's sleep. Exercise caution when it comes to caffeine, and choose sensibly depending on your body's reaction to it.

Manage Stress Levels

Stress is one of the worst causes of memory problems and other brain-related issues. Chronic stress can destroy and damage brain cells and the hippocampus area resulting in problems associated with new memories and consolidation. Here are some stress-management tips:

- Set yourself realistic expectations and learn to

say no when you cannot take on more than what you have on your plate
- Take short relaxing breaks right through the day
- Don't bottle up your emotions; express them openly
- Balance work and leisure sensibly
- Avoid Multitasking; it drains your brain power and results in reduced efficiency

Another effective way to reduce stress is to laugh more. Here are some tips to make sure you increase the laughter and joy in your life:

'Laughter is the best medicine' is an old but timeless cliché, which is good for the memory too. Studies have shown that laughter affects multiple regions of the brain stimulating it much more than other emotional responses. Additionally, jokes and punch lines are creative and listening to them can stimulate your creative thinking ability too. Here are some ways to improve laughter in your life:

Laugh at yourself – One of the most effective

ways to convert serious moments in our life is to find something funny in it, and laugh it off. This approach to laughing at the difficult and embarrassing aspects of our life will teach us to look at everything around us with joy, happiness, and laughter.

Move toward laughter – Allow yourself to be attracted by laughter. Whenever and wherever you hear laughter, gravitate toward it and share and laugh about the joke. Sharing something innocently (without rancor or malafide intent to hurt) funny by anybody is an opportunity to laugh.

Surround yourself with happy people – Happiness is contagious and so is sadness. Being around morose and sad people will affect you too. Avoid them as much as you can, or at least, consciously avoid being affected by their depressive attitude. Instead, surround yourself with happy people who never lose an opportunity to laugh.

Pay attention to children's behavior – Children are the most unaffected by the vagaries of life, and what they exhibit is the truest form of emotion that can be seen. Look at children's behaviors and you will notice that they can laugh and find joy in anything around them. Try and emulate them as much as you can.

Make time for your family, friends, and loved ones – If you thought that only serious mental and challenging mental exercises can help you boost your memory, think again. Being around your loved ones in a happy atmosphere is also known to boost memory.

Human beings are social animals. We are not meant to live in isolation. Forget thriving, even surviving in isolation is not easy for us. Relationships, friends, and family stimulate our brains, and human interaction could, perhaps, be the best and the most effective form of mental exercises.

Research studies have proven that strong

emotional relationships are not just good for the heart but also for the brain. So, always find time to be amongst loving people who care for and love you. Warm relationships are good for your memory.

More Memory Building Tips

Mnemonics – Remember the school grade mnemonic VIBGYOR to remember the seven colors of the rainbow? Using mnemonics is a powerful tool to remember and recall information from your long-term memory. Here are some examples:

Expression mnemonics or acronyms – **MY VERY EDUCATED MOTHER JUST SERVED US NINE PIZZAS** is a mnemonic that stands for the nine planets in our solar system. The first letter of each word gives the starting letter of the planet's name from Mercury (My) to Pluto (Pizzas). **EVERY GOOD BOY DOES FINE** is an acronym for the treble clef EGBDF (in music).

Music Mnemonics – music can be used to create powerful mnemonics because they are easily repeatable, engaging, and fun. It is so much easier to remember a catchy tune instead of a long string of plain words or texts. Look at all the old school rhymes that you used to learn the alphabets or the song for the elements in the periodic table.

You can create your own song based on a favorite tune. Even the act of creating the song will help in improving your memory through creativity.

Chunking Technique – Another form of mnemonics is to chunk information together. For example, if you have to remember a telephone number like 9995550660, you would most likely say 999 555 0660. This is chunking similar data together thereby increasing your ability to remember.

In the chunking technique, you group similar items together, finding some kind of pattern in them, and then organize them in a way that is logical and structure for easy memory and recall. For example, in your grocery list, you can group together the times that are found in one aisle. When you are learning history, you can look for connections between the various events during a particular period, and chunk them together.

Chunking techniques work very well because by default our brains look for patterns and connect them together. Our memory works efficiently and effectively to draw information from raw data and find logical patterns by using refined methods of chunking. Here are some examples where chunking techniques will work very well:

- If you have a long list to remember, group similar items together, and form small groups of lists within the big list.
- If the list consists of vocabulary words, then create small groups of similar or related words
- Break your grocery list into fruit list, vegetable list, grain list, dairy list, and so forth.

Make Handwritten Notes of Information – Put away your computer, and revert to making handwritten notes for critical information that you need to remember and recall later on. There are many reasons why handwritten notes are preferable over typing out notes on the computer. Here are some reasons why:

- The act of writing stimulates specific brain cells located at the base and referred to a reticular activating system (RAS). The brain is known to focus more when the RAS is activated. Therefore, when your hand is physically making notes, your brain is more active as it follows the movement of your hand as it forms each letter, which enhances your memory and cognitive skills.
- Research studies have also proven that people who handwrite their lectures are able to deliver them verbatim whereas people who type the lectures out invariably paraphrase the ideas during the class.

So, always try and make handwritten notes as

much as possible. Mind maps are useful handwritten notes because you don't have to write long-drawn sentences, and yet, can leverage the advantage of handwriting.

Repetition – How many times have you learned something for a test, and promptly forgotten it almost immediately? Unless we compel our brains to work actively and retained the learned information, we will lose what we have learned. If you want to remember information in the long-term horizon, then you have to vocalize and learn it repeatedly.

Spaced repetition is considered the most efficient way of repeatedly learning. After you have learned something new, you take a short break (2-3 days) and learn it again. Keep increasing this break from 2-3 days to 1-2 weeks to 1-2 months to 6 months as the data gets deeply imbibed into your brain. You can make handwritten notes on flashcards, and use them for this spaced repetition learning.

Conclusion

Learning memory techniques will not just help you pass a test or find your car keys or help you make a grocery list or some such mundane thing. These techniques improve your memory, which has lifelong benefits. With a great memory, you can easily achieve the following:

- Get great grades in school
- Get promotions at work easily because you will be able to recall and follow instructions to the T
- People in sales can do very well with great memory skills as they can recall names of their customers with ease endearing them for life
- Your personal relationships will improve thanks to your ability to remember birthdays, anniversaries, and other important days in the life of your friends and family, and of course, your spouse

- Effects of aging are first felt in the brain. Memory techniques help in staving off the aging process in the brain keeping you mentally sharp and alert even when you are old

Therefore, memory techniques don't just give you productivity and efficiency but also happiness and joy as you learn to live your life in a more fulfilling and meaningful way than before.

www.ingramcontent.com/pod-product-compliance
Lightning Source LLC
LaVergne TN
LVHW010410070526
838199LV00065B/5934